IQBAL
AND HIS INGENIOUS
IDEA

To my scientists, Josh and Emma. Here's to your ingenious ideas! — E.S.
To the ladies at The Warren — R.G.

Acknowledgments

Thanks to the Global Alliance for Clean Cookstoves (cleancookstoves.org) and Solar Cookers International (SCI) (solarcookers.org) for information about the multiple benefits of clean cooking. The Global Alliance is a public–private partnership hosted by the United Nations Foundation to save lives, improve livelihoods, empower women and protect the environment. The mission of SCI is to spread solar thermal cooking technology to benefit people and environments. To learn more about these organizations, please visit their websites.

Thanks as well to Rebecca and the entire KCP publishing team. I couldn't ask for a more collaborative, creative and socially conscious group to work with.

Kids Can Press gratefully acknowledges the financial support of the Government of Ontario, through the Ontario Media Development Corporation, for our publishing activity.

Published in Canada and the U.S. by Kids Can Press Ltd.
25 Dockside Drive, Toronto, ON M5A 0B5

Kids Can Press is a Corus Entertainment Inc. company

www.kidscanpress.com

The artwork in this book was rendered in colored pencil and edited digitally. The text is set in Cronos Pro.

Edited by Stacey Roderick and Katie Scott
Designed by Marie Bartholomew

Printed and bound in Malaysia
in 10/2017 by Tien Wah Press (Pte.) Ltd.

CM 18 0 9 8 7 6 5 4 3 2 1

Library and Archives Canada Cataloguing in Publication

Suneby, Elizabeth, 1958–, author

Iqbal and his ingenious idea : how a science project helps one family and the planet / written by Elizabeth Suneby ; illustrated by Rebecca Green.

(CitizenKid)
ISBN 978-1-77138-720-0 (hardcover)

1. Air — Pollution — Juvenile fiction. 2. Air — Pollution — Health aspects — Juvenile fiction. 3. Air quality management — Juvenile fiction. 4. Solar ovens — Juvenile fiction. I. Green, Rebecca, 1986–, illustrator II. Title. III. Series: CitizenKid

PZ7.S9145Iq 2018   j813'.6   C2017-903192-9

IQBAL
AND HIS INGENIOUS
IDEA

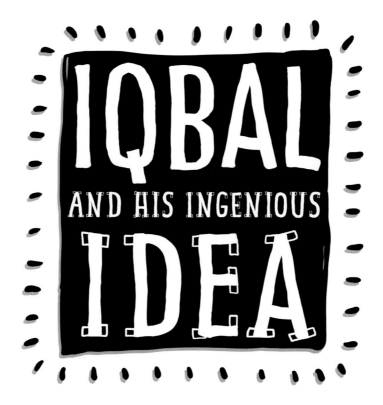

HOW A SCIENCE PROJECT
HELPS ONE FAMILY
AND THE PLANET

ELIZABETH SUNEBY
REBECCA GREEN

CitizenKid™

A collection of books that inform children about the world and inspire them to be better global citizens

KIDS CAN PRESS

IQBAL and his friends stepped out of their school and into the rain. Not a light mist or even a steady downpour, but gusts of rain that whip across your face and make you squint your eyes. Monsoon rain.

"Hurry, Iqbal!" called his sister. Sadia stood clutching her umbrella as she waited at their after-school meeting spot.

At home, Iqbal and Sadia's mother stirred a pot of rice, a baby swaddled against her. "Sadia," said Amma, over the baby's raspy cough, "please take Rupa to the veranda. The smoke is bothering her."

Iqbal sat down beside his mother. "Amma, my teacher told us the theme for this year's district science fair. It's sustainability. We have a month to come up with a project that's good for the environment. There are cash prizes for the winner and the runner-up!"

From the veranda, Sadia overheard her brother and yelled out, "Iqbal, let me be your assistant. Then you'll win!"

Amma chuckled as she shooed Iqbal out the door. It was the holy month of Ramadan, and he was meeting his father for evening prayers.

As Iqbal hurried off, Amma muffled a cough. Day after day of breathing smoke was making both her and the baby sick. But during monsoon rains, she had no choice but to cook indoors over an open fire.

After the family's evening meal, Amma rested. Tomorrow she would need to take Rupa and go out to gather firewood. Their supply was low.

As Amma dozed, Iqbal's father whispered, "I saw a special stove at the bazaar today. The man selling it says it uses propane gas, so it doesn't create all the smoke that is making Amma and the baby sick."

"Can't we get one, Abba?" Iqbal asked.

"We don't have the money," his father said with a sigh. "I wish we did."

That night, Iqbal fell asleep to the sound of rain drumming on the tin roof. But soon he was awakened by Amma's and Rupa's coughing. He tossed and turned, worrying about them. To distract himself, he tried thinking of a winning project for the science fair.

In fact, he thought about the science fair a lot in the following days.

He imagined inventions while walking to and from school with Sadia.

He sketched all sorts of gadgets in between classes.

He conceived of contraptions when helping Abba in the rice paddy.

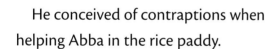

He dreamed about devices before and after his daily prayers.
Finally, he came up with a winning idea. He would build a stove
that didn't produce smoke!

At school the next day, Iqbal explained the idea to his teacher. They went straight to the computer in the office and typed in "smokeless cooking." Up popped articles about solar stoves that cook with the heat of the sun.

He learned that solar cookers don't pollute the air. They also save women from having to collect wood and cook over dangerous flames.

Iqbal realized that Amma could use a solar cooker during Bangladesh's five sunny seasons. And with the prize money, Abba could buy the gas stove he saw at the bazaar to use indoors during the monsoon season.

SOLAR COOKER

PROTECTS +HE ENVIRONMENT
REDUCES HEALTH PROBLEMS
EMPOWERS WOMEN AND GIRLS
INCREASES SAFETY
SAVES MONEY

NO: BURNING WOOD   OPEN FLAMES
    AIR POLLUTION   ELECTRICITY

Iqbal brought home the best articles he had found about how to build a solar cooker and started reading.

"Let me help," said Sadia, grabbing a couple. "Remember, I am your assistant."

Within seconds, Sadia exclaimed, "Look, look at this! Solar cookers made from cardboard boxes covered in foil."

Iqbal didn't look up.

She tried getting her brother's attention again — "Iqbal, these stoves use the sun's heat." And again — "Iqbal, are you listening to me?"

He wasn't. Iqbal was too excited by his own discovery. "Here's our winner, Sadia — a solar cooker made from an umbrella!" Every family they knew had an old umbrella or two that had been broken by the gusty monsoon winds.

To make their umbrella cooker, Sadia and Iqbal removed
the handle from the biggest broken umbrella they could find.
Abba gave them money to buy foil to cover the top of the
umbrella. And since dark colors hold heat best, they borrowed
one of Amma's old soot-blackened pans to cook in.

Now all they needed was a few sunny hours to test their
invention.

But it rained the next day. And the day after. And the day
after that. They wondered if the rain would ever stop.

Finally, it did. The first day that the clouds parted and the sun brightened the sky, Sadia and Iqbal bought eggs at the bazaar and raced home.

They carefully positioned the foil-covered umbrella to catch the sun's rays, placed the pan inside and waited. And waited.

Iqbal sprinkled a drop of water into the pan. "Not ready yet," he said. He counted slowly to fifty — "ēk, dui, tin ..." — and tried again. The bead of water skittered across the bottom. "It's hot!" he exclaimed.

Sadia cracked an egg on the edge of the pan, and it slithered into the middle. They watched and waited some more.

"Look!" Iqbal yelled. "Amma, come quick! We are frying an egg for you!"

A couple of weeks later, it was the event Iqbal and his classmates had been waiting for — the announcement of the science-fair winners. The students lined up behind their projects. One of them had won first prize for the entire district. But who?

Was it Rashad and his experiment to reduce soil erosion?

How about Tareq with his wind turbine?

Maybe Rafee had won for his compost container?

Or … Iqbal for his solar cooker?

The principal entered the room and began his speech: "Thank you, students, for all your hard work."

Iqbal's heart pounded.

The principal continued, "One student has come up with a particularly ingenious idea. He saved a broken umbrella from the garbage dump and turned it into a fried egg."

The class giggled.

He went on, "Smoke from cooking fires is a big problem in our country. It pollutes the air and causes health problems, especially for women and small children."

The principal placed the ribbon on Iqbal's solar cooker and shook the boy's hand. He had won first prize!

After weeks of rain, bright days finally outnumbered gray ones. Monsoon season had come to an end. And so had Ramadan.

Using the winning umbrella cooker and the new gas stove purchased with Iqbal's prize money, Amma and Sadia had been busy cooking for Eid al-Fitr, the feast to celebrate the end of the holy month.

Abba handed his son the first serving of the family's favorite sweet dish, *semai*. Iqbal passed it to Sadia. After all, she really had been an excellent assistant.

ABOUT CLEAN COOKSTOVES

This fictional story is based on the experiences of many people living in densely populated Bangladesh, a country located near the northeastern corner of India on the Bay of Bengal. Like Iqbal's family in the story, most Bangladeshi people cook their food over open fires. This contributes to the air pollution that affects the health of many millions of people and causes tens of thousands of deaths annually in that country. In fact, around the world three billion people cook over open fires or on stoves that burn air-polluting solid fuels, such as wood or coal. Many of these people live in sub-Saharan Africa or South Asia.

The good news is that "clean cookstoves" — stoves that don't cause pollution and/or that use efficient fuels — are available. Clean cookers offer several benefits, including these:

• **Protecting the environment** — Less black carbon, greenhouse gas and other pollutants are released into the environment, which reduces air pollution, climate change, deforestation and loss of biodiversity.

• **Reducing health problems** — These cookers decrease the pollution that causes more than four million untimely deaths every year and contributes to many serious health problems, such as pneumonia, stroke, lung cancer, heart disease, asthma, low birth weight and skin burns.

• **Empowering women and girls** — Reducing the hard and dangerous work of cooking over open fires and the time needed for collecting fuel, which are typically the responsibilities of women and girls, allows the female members of the household to spend more time with their families, pursue an education or earn income.

• **Increasing safety** — Women and girls no longer need to cook over dangerous flames or travel long distances, sometimes into unsafe areas, to gather fuel.

In the story, Iqbal discovers a clean-cooking option that uses the sun's energy to heat up and cook food. Solar cookstoves, or solar cookers, work well in areas where the sun shines most days, including countries located near the equator. Some families in these countries use other clean-cooking solutions, including the gas stove that Iqbal's father sees at the bazaar, in addition to solar cooking, which is a slow-cooking method.

Pizza Box Solar Cooker Instructions

Iqbal's ingenious idea was to use an umbrella to turn sunlight into heat energy and make a solar cooker. You can make your own solar cooker using an empty pizza box. A hot, sunny day — at least 29.5°C (85°F) — is best. Be sure that you have an adult helping you who will do the cutting with the utility knife.

You will need:

• a clean pizza box

• aluminum foil

• clear plastic wrap

• a sheet of black construction paper

• a wooden stick, such as a skewer

• a pencil or pen, ruler, utility knife, glue stick and electrical tape

• s'mores ingredients: graham crackers, marshmallows and a chocolate bar

1. Using the ruler, draw a square on top of the lid of the closed pizza box, about 2.5 cm (1 in.) from the sides.

2. Carefully cut along three sides of the square to make a flap. (Be sure not to cut the side closest to the fold.) Fold back the flap.

3. Cover the inside of the flap with aluminum foil (shiny side out). Making sure the foil is as smooth as possible, glue down the edges. (It's okay if the foil wraps around the edges of the flap.)

4. Stretch plastic wrap over the opening in the lid (where you cut out the flap) and tape it in place. There should be no holes in the plastic.

5. Cover the inside of the box bottom with foil (shiny side up). Again making sure the foil is smooth, glue down the edges.

6. Cut a 10 cm (4 in.) square from the black paper. Center it in the bottom of the box (now covered in foil) and glue it down. This is where you will place your food.

7. Using the wooden stick, prop open the flap to about a 60-degree angle.

On a hot, sunny, windless day, place your oven out in the sun, with your s'mores inside the box on the black paper. Position the box so that the sunlight is reflected from the flap into the box. As the aluminum foil heats up, be careful not to touch it! You should start to notice the chocolate melting after about 30 to 40 minutes.

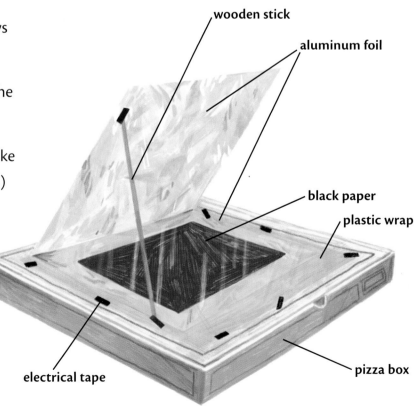

Words in italics are in Bengali, the official language of Bangladesh.

Abba (AH-bah): Father

Amma (AH-mah): Mother

dui (do-ee): two

Eid al-Fitr (EED ool-FEE-tur): the important Muslim holiday that marks the end of Ramadan

ēk (ACK): one

monsoon: powerful seasonal winds that bring heavy rainfall

propane: a type of gas commonly used for cooking

Ramadan: the holy month for people of the Muslim faith, observed by fasting from sunrise to sunset, introspection and prayer

semai (SHEM-eye): a popular dessert eaten at Eid al-Fitr that is made with vermicelli noodles, milk, ghee (clarified butter) and sugar

sustainability: processes and systems that do not deplete Earth's natural resources or damage the environment and living beings

tin (THEEN): three